Anticipated Eternity

I0086644

Exhale Taop

To my son; for teaching me what love
is.

To Joshua Williams (Cozy Creatives);
for the illustrations and helping me
bring my vision to life .

CONTENTS

Budding

I put you in my diary.
On a page where
my secrets and truths
take refuge.
As if seeking shade
from your sun
beneath a willow tree;
that I would love
to carve our initials into.
But you don't know me.
You see I've been
admiring you from a distance.
I built a telescope
to study every star in your constellation.
Only to discover that you're a galaxy.

Let's collide
like cosmic colors
and create an explosion
that will leave the world in awe.

We
could
make
so
much
magic.

We could take off running
towards the horizon and crash.

Right into where
the sun meets the land.

And then we could

fly
        fly
                fly.

Just to pass the time.

You look like you taste of
chocolate and daydreams.

You seep from the pores of my mind.
Like honey.
Oozing from its comb.
Slow & sweet.

How I wish to be
inside that smile.

I only see you.

The brightest light upon mountain peaks
with rivers that flow just as smoothly as you do.

I bet the sun peeks through your blinds
just to shine
on that melanin.

I wanna write love songs on your skin.

Have you ever looked into your eyes?

There's more in there than this dimension has to offer.

I wish I were a tree in Autumn so you would
stop and admire my leaves. Mimicking the
sunrise to your satisfaction. Which shade of
falls transformation do you prefer? If you stood
beneath my canopy I would shower you. First
in canary yellow, soft like feathers on skin.
Then in marigold orange, a warmth to
encourage our blossom. And finally crimson,
a red to fuse with what runs through your
veins. How does it feel, drowning in my
reverie? You see I fantasize about you.
The way your lips would part if they said my
name. Or the hue of brown your eyes are in the
sunlight. Or how fast your heart would beat if I
kissed you. Simple dreams, some
indescribable. Like how I assume the skin on
your back would feel beneath my fingernails.
Or how you could touch my soul from the
space between my hips. And how I would just
melt for you. You see these fantasies and
dreams are starting to sprout like leaves.
Desperate to fall down from a tree that grew
only in order to seek, your admiration.
But its only Summer.

The thought of you thinking of me.

I wanna be the craters in your moon.
Engraved into you.
Surrounded by S T A R S.
But they don't twinkle like you do.

Can we spin
around
run
and lie down in the rain?

I just wanna
dance
with you
off beat.

Let's stargaze
from balconies
roofs
and fields of daisies.

I wanna put that pressure on you.

If I make the shea butter
I rubbed in
drip from my skin
like juice
onto your lips
until your thirst
is quenched…

Will I be your favorite flavor?

And if I let you slide
inside
the space
between my thighs
where nectar spills
from my walls
while you climb…

Can I call you mine?

Forever.

Blooming

Sweat glands drip
as a piece of my past rips.
I am new.
The sun rises and you taste
like morning dew.
Wind blows green grass,
and the tempo our heart beats make.
The rhythm our souls create.
We are one as our lips collide
we freeze in time and explode.
Please exhale the smoke.
An overdose of perfection.
I'm caught in your essence.
A kaleidoscope of dreams.
Follow me on the path I lead
to the blue enigma tree.
The art of persuasion,
beauty beyond reality.
Take my hand.
We may never understand.
You cant decipher love
but we can devise a plan.
Lets run away.
Such a sweet escape.
Fairytale paradise.
No destination in sight.

I
was
watching
my heart fall
before you caught it.

I discover new constellations
every time I look at you.

       And I swear you're sparkling with them.

I hold you while I sleep
so you know who I dream of.

I'm ingesting your anatomy.
Conversing with your molecules
about eternity.

I fall inside your eyes.

When I look at you I see
magic dripping from your pores.

Your heart pumps light into your veins.

Baby you're luminescent.

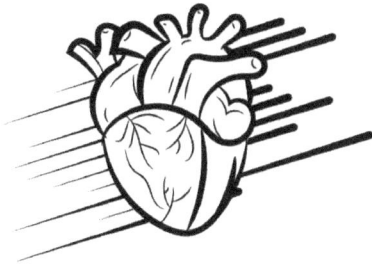

The smoothness of your skin
is like poetry on my tongue.

I love the way you touch my mind, tracing one brain cell at a time. Removing my inhibitions and setting them aside. Intent on aligning the stars in your eyes with mine... Just so we could shine together.

And I know we could storm the weather. Wind or snow, for worse or better. I wanna rain on you, leave my morning dew on your petals.

Your
name
is
sweet
on
my
tongue.
It
drips
from
my
lips
like
pineapple
juice.

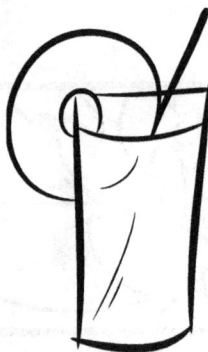

May I marinate in the
depths of your womb?
Is home still where the heart is
if my heart is in you?
Penetrating your layers like razors
from the grenade
my insecurities threw.
A collision of atoms as our lips touched
but I never could trust
that mine were the only ones
you were attached to.

The sincerity in your eyes
battled the uncertainty
in your gestures.
The dark sky fought the sunrise
at the peak of dawn
for a beauty love
couldn't even measure.
As my soul yearned to spill feelings
that go beyond 26 letters.

Your skin plays as a symphony
engulfing me like black velvet sheets.
I drown in the sound your fingertips leave.
With your words as soft as rose petals
my mental melts like falling stars.
Mysterious like the silhouettes that
your absence engraved into my heart.

The taste your warmth makes
controls the tempo of my pulse.
Tainting my bloodstream
with the rhythm of your soul.
We dance as royals
while my anticipation grows.
Suspended in the truth
our tell tale hearts never told.

And suddenly you break free
chasing the flame
that flickers in my eyes.
Wishing only to prove to me
that that flame is the burnt orange
that caresses your horizon.

We are only as far apart
as the eye can see.
Follow the passion that's
painted in the sky.
Your lips speak against
the doubts I breathe
as our molecules
and legs intertwine.

So I marinate in the
depths of your womb
For home is where the heart is
and my heart is in you.

Sun rays caress the shadows through cracked curtains. Illuminating dust particles. Falling, often twinkling. A slight glimmer in your eyes. They're unreal. Resembling those of a porcelain doll. Mine leading you on a voyage

as you dare to meet my gaze. We are here yet I feel taken away. Far from you minus the distance. We are together almost as one. Your hand is gentle in its exploration. Discovering the perfection within the flaws of my skin. From my cheek to the base of my neck. My body softens at your touch. Your fingertips trace my inhibitions. A sweet release as our hands meet. Fingers interlace. Mold. Mine made specifically for the space between yours. Captivation. Lost in time. It is not the moon that illuminates the room. My body. All of who I am. Lost in your arms. Seized. Captured. Trapped. Your hands settled upon the crease of my lower back. Lift my head from doubt. Cheeks in your palms. A sweet remedy. I lift my eyes. Your lips sweep my forehead. A whisper breaks the silence. My ears crinkle to the sound of "I love you." My heart loses its beat. It finds yours. My soul trembles. A depth being filled. Passion collides. Our lips collaborate in a tantalizing melody. Secretes revealed in the warmth of our melting sorrows. And we stay here. Never to retreat. Even as the darkness of war sends call. Forever we fight. Entangled in a beautiful disaster. Between sheets. Creating. Sculpting. Making love. Nothing could tear us apart. Anticipated eternity in a battle of the hearts.

Wilting

Her petals were falling.

I've been on this quest for a while now.
Settling for temporary optical illusions of love.
But remember when I found you?
We're both wanderers.
Journeys put on hold
to admire the sunflowers.
Dying to match their patience and longevity.
We started spreading like vines and wildfire.
Engulfing everything around us.
But there was still something missing.

You used to kiss me
like your second chance
at life was in my lips.

I'm watching all the colors
of love fall out of the sky.

Your heart is iridescent.

I'm paralyzed and all the grays
feel warmer than they used to.

Why are you running that way?

Why can't I chase you?

There's a puddle of red left where I stand
but our grass was never green to begin with.

I remember all the purple flames.

How they danced around us.

I couldn't even see you
through the smoke but
I wasn't afraid to breathe.

Inhaling the fumes as we combusted.

We were ethereal.

I try to run from it
but I don't have a choice
than to embrace the
after taste of our memories.

And of course it was perfect. Turtle doves form a heart as he unties her corset. A barrier released as her body starts to fidget. But he easers her pain and stops her intuition. Starts up her heart. Beat racing through inhibitions.
Killing her softly. A beautiful disaster being written. Beyond smitten. More than bad religion. The unforeseen future of a past with no revisions.

And of course it was perfect. Turtle doves form a heart. He treats her body like a portrait.
But her mental not so art had him ready to forfeit. As the stitches they wove start to unravel that corset.

But they knew it wasn't perfect. Turtle doves fly away. Leaving feathers at your doorstep. One for each wish and prayer they come back. But the wind blows them away. Leaving your perception of perfection abstract

The room still smells like you.

And I haven't really tried to change that.

I still
feel your
spark on
my lips.

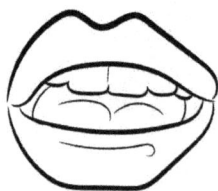

I loved you.
I loved you like flowers love sunshine.
Yearning to grow into something
just as beautiful as sunrise.
Or like birds love song.
Singing freedom into the trees
until the wind sings along.
Like the waves love sand.
Never getting tired of crashing
into each other over and over again.
I loved you like fire loves to burn.
Choking on the ashes from the
trust you never earned.
My lungs go back to black
because we only said goodbye with words.
But my heart knows its real
so I can't hide from the hurt.
And I know I should move on
because you weren't what I'm worth.
But I can't because I loved you
like mother loves Earth.
I loved you like rainbows love the storm.
Promising forgiveness for the damage
that was done.
I loved you.
More than any words I could speak
But it doesn't matter
because you never loved me.

We were a flower
that could not bloom.
We were trapped in a vase.
Our roots had no room
to grow.

I drowned in you again and again.
Never once wishing to learn how to swim.
I just kept sinking and breathing you in.
You were my oxygen.

We were like waves.

We crashed.

We caved.

I
tried
to
make
you
love
me.

Your fingertips left streaks.

Residue from an attempted masterpiece.

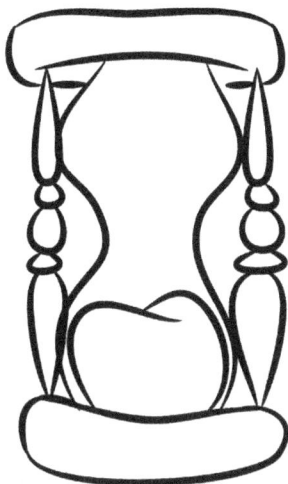

Thank you for reading this, for making it to this page. Thank you for falling inside my thoughts and spending time with me.

"Could've been anywhere in the world but you here with me! That's good for my egoooo"
- Kanye West

I hope I made you feel me.

ABOUT THE AUTHOR

Exhale Taop makes her debut as a self-published author with *Anticipated Eternity.*

"I was inspired to write poetry in a middle school English class, and never looked back."

Fast forward 10 years and Exhale is not only a mother and an author, but a recording/performing artist in North Carolina. With her career as a music artist continuing to grow, Exhale decided to shine light on her other creative ventures, to give her supporters a feel for who she truly is as an artist.

"It's words in general. I like words, and using them to make people feel. I wanted to show people that I am more than a 'rapper'. It's also a goal of mine to show people that we do reap the fruits of our labor. I am a 'regular' person, pursuing dreams I could've left in my sleep, and I am achieving them. And you can too!"

For more from Exhale you can visit
www.exhaletaop.com
Instagram: exhaletaop **Facebook:** Exhale TAOP
YouTube: Exhale TAOP